MY 'GREAT RESIGNATION'

A FRESHER'S REAL LIFE ANECDOTE REVOLVING AROUND HIS FIRST CORPORATE JOB !

AKSHAY PRATAP SINGH

Made with ♥ on the Notion Press Platform
www.notionpress.com

To my parents and my sisters, the silent architects of my dreams, who instilled in me the courage to embrace change and the resilience to navigate uncharted territories. Your unwavering support has been the cornerstone of my journey, and I dedicate this book, "My Great Resignation," to the foundation you've built within me.

Contents

Foreword

In the pages that follow, Akshay invites us into a world shaped by the intricate dance between professional aspirations and personal growth. "My Great Resignation" is not merely a chronicle of corporate life but a profound exploration of the human spirit. As we embark on this literary journey, the author's narrative unfolds with a rare blend of vulnerability and strength. It is a tale of embracing change, confronting challenges, and finding solace in the support of loved ones. In Akshay's words, we discover a mosaic of resilience, positive mindset, love, and unwavering support that transcends the boundaries of the corporate realm. This book is an invitation to reflect on our own stories, finding common ground in the universal themes of perseverance and growth.

Preface

As I pen down the preface to "My Great Resignation," I am humbled by the privilege of sharing my journey with you, dear reader. This book emerged from the amalgamation of personal reflections, professional challenges, and the unyielding spirit of resilience. It is an ode to the twists and turns that life presents, a testament to the power of a positive mindset, and an acknowledgment of the love and support that have illuminated my path. Within these pages, you will find not just my story but echoes of your own experiences. So, let us embark on this shared exploration of triumphs, setbacks, and the ceaseless pursuit of growth.

Acknowledgements

In the tapestry of "My Great Resignation," numerous threads have been woven together, and it is with profound gratitude that I acknowledge those who have played pivotal roles in this literary endeavor.

To my parents, whose love and guidance have been the compass guiding me through uncharted waters, I express my deepest appreciation. Your unwavering belief in my journey has been the wind beneath my wings.

To my elder sisters and friends, you have been the pillars of support in my virtual and real-world endeavors. Your encouragement and feedback have enriched every word of my articles, blogs, and now, this book. I am grateful for the shared laughter, challenges, and triumphs.

To my online readers, the silent audience whose love has fueled my passion for storytelling, I extend my heartfelt thanks. Your virtual presence has been a constant source of inspiration, motivating me to bring this narrative to life.

With sincere appreciation, I extend my gratitude to all those who have contributed to the making of "My Great Resignation." May this book resonate with the shared experiences of its readers, fostering a sense of connection and understanding in the vast tapestry of human stories.

Prologue

Distressed and perturbed, I came back to my home after office. The sun had set just now and so was the motive of my life. The lights were on, the curtains opened but the fresh breeze of spring couldn't help even. Year back the same day, I was enjoying this job. What had really made the difference was still the question of the hour.

I unbuttoned my office uniform and slipped into the bathroom to have a quick shower. The sprinkles were stress relieving but lasted as long as I was under the shower. *Akshay, you should have talked to him. Why did you let him go?*

I came out of the shower and wet the floor with a half-drenched body. I changed into my comfy tee and pyjamas and comforted myself on the bed. Lights were blocking my thoughts so I chose to turn off all of them except the one coming from the bathroom. Besides my bed was a window which opened the sight more into a dramatic scene of cinema rather than a cluster of houses. The sideways balcony gave a picture of a middle aged woman shouting over her eight year old son for not completing the school work while the front facing house had a different picture. A four year old girl was nonchalantly putting her body weight over the railings of the balcony, enjoying the realms of that season. The only thing common between the two houses was the serenity and calmness of either of the houses. But it wasn't the situation of this flat which a year ago I had turned into a home.

Opposite to my window was a wall which had a tree wallpaper with sticky notes on each of its branches. Each sticky note had a message written on it, which was addressed to me by my very own hands. "You are doing a great job", "You nailed it", "Never let yourself down", etc. Beside the wallpaper, hung a whiteboard which had few plans and rough flowcharts for my upcoming projects. The other side of my room had an almirah stacked with Puma, UCB, Adidas, etc. I bought all those branded clothes with my very own hard earned money, for I loved wearing brands. Attached with almirah was a table too which had multiple collections of novels. Dan Brown, Agatha Christie, you name any. I barely missed reading any of the latest fiction. Last year when I moved into this flat, I made this a home all by myself. Every corner of this room has become a part of my life since then.

6:30 has ticked in the evening and under the darkness of that dusk, I am lying with the laments of my professional life. It felt like that this job stress was eating me from inside like a termite. And, today it felt worse. I can hear my soul shrilling from inside and I needed to make a final decision today.

Suddenly, my phone rang and it's my manager. *Oh Akshay! Best chance, talk to him.* Still ringing. I swiped up the green button.

"He..llo..Hello sir?"

"Akshay?? You're okay? What happened to your voice?"

"Sir.. I was.."

"We have something to discuss. A meeting has suddenly popped up for the coming morning. We need to be prepared for it. Can you please spare some 30 minutes in the night to prepare? We can connect on teams!"

"Okay sir," I disconnected.

Call was hung up but I guess I have got the message. All my laments were blown up. I got up from my bed, put off my specs and went to the bathroom, this time, to wash my tears. With firm hands, I splashed the water hard on my face, looked straight into the mirror and nodded, "GO!"

No! No preparations for the morning meeting now. I was firm. I took my phone and opened my manager's chat box in Whatsapp.

"Sir, it's very tough to work in this environment. At times, I feel running out of energy. The expectations are too high, the resources way too less. This has become a daily fashion and I literally feel both demotivated and exhausted. I have tried reaching the higher management but I can't seek any support.

I am afraid sir if I can continue like this!"

Sent.

CHAPTER ONE

New Joinee

"Akshay, it's final! You are joining the Supply Chain segment. I hope you were satisfied with the department allotment," the HR gave me an ultimatum. I fake smiled and decided to go with the flow. Although, I preferred core manufacturing in the choices but this was it. It didn't matter. I was in no way serious about this job.

"And the department you'll look into is, Purchase!" she added. Again, my fake smiles continued because it didn't matter. "Sharp 2PM, your Head will connect with you. Just a short meeting. Please be ready!" she ended.

Post lunch when the clock showed 1:55 in the noon, I was lying on my bed with a laptop beside a cookie packet. Lousy and sleepy, I was waiting for the head to show up. As the clock showed 1:59, I improved my sitting posture and slid my hairs well to look decent and professional. Just then, a noise came out from Teams. Someone has joined the meeting. Head has joined the meeting. Big round specs, dark black thick moustaches and a pot belly. He looked like a proper *Laala* of some business, although his personality and mannerism spoke a lot about his good education as well.

"Hey Akshay! How are you?"

"Good noon sir. I am good."

"So, ready for the new phase of life? Supply chain won't be that easy," he giggled.

"Sir, I love challenges!" I giggled back.

"Great..great! How is your relationship with numbers?" he asked.

"Oh! I love them so much that I never scored below 90 in both maths & computers," I boasted.

"Hmmm.." he started pondering and continued asking some more questions.

There were some more questions about my hobbies and passion. We talked for the next 10 minutes. It was the end of the session and what he said surprised me a bit.

"Akshay, I am asking HR to assign you Planning. You are a Planning guy not the Purchase guy." He smiled.

"Sure sir. No issues," and the meeting ended.

WTF is Planning now? But how does it matter? I didn't care for Purchase either.

I didn't know this 10 minute conversation would change my life forever.

Moving into Office

It was the winter of 2020. We were enjoying both the Autumn and Diwali festival but it was few days later only that we were asked to come and join the office. Post covid era it was, people were strictly following the protocols of 'Wear your mask' but the so called 'Social distancing' was a mere fallacy.

It was the 18th of November when I first entered my office. A warehouse stacked full of cardboard boxes with automotive parts fairly wrapped inside them. Up above the warehouse was an office full of a supply chain team.

A regular-fit blue check shirt, greyish blue pants, black shiny shoes and an ID card hung loose around my neck. Yes, this was me! A fresher well dressed, climbing the staircase to enter his office life.

On entering the office on first floor, it felt like I entered a share market place. Phone calls, roars, people running from here and there and what not? For a moment, I was flabbergasted.

"Where can I meet Vikas Mungee?" I asked one of the guys sitting adjacent to the entrance. He pinpointed a person sitting in the middle talking to someone over the phone. I recognized him through our previous online sessions. He looked very stressed in person. Seems like the work pressure has overwhelmed him too much. After all, he was in this department for the past 10 years.

Vikas immediately recognized me and greeted me with a smile.

"Hi Akshay! Come, sit here." He ushered me to his adjacent chair.

"Hi sir."

"So?? First time being in Indore? I'll suggest some really good places to explore here." He urged.

I nodded with affirmation.

"You can look around the warehouse today. We won't be having any sessions today since I am already piled up with a lot of work," he finished.

Next, I was roaming around in the warehouse without showing a little bit of interest. I started phone calling my friends and would have long conversations with my college friends. And that is how my first day passed in a jiffy. From the next day onwards, my new colleague, Vikas Mungee, started teaching me the ropes of planning. Mind you, I was a really nasty guy. I wasn't showing any interest in what he was teaching me. Although, I would jot down everything in the form of notes.

With time, I started taking the tasks under my bucket. They felt too mundane and boring. At times, I would crib about the work I was doing. I wouldn't understand even the ABCD of supply chain but I would still continue finishing the work due to cumbersome deadlines. This went for like another month and we were in the starting of 2021.

Big Project coming up

"So, is he in your team?" The tall man in front of me asked Vikas.

"Yes, he recently joined us. He's especially called for this project.." Vikas laughed in a fashion and introduced me to the person.

"Akshay, he is Tushar Sinha. He'll be our consultant for this project." We shook hands.

Tushar was some 6 feet tall guy, wearing some really expensive white shirt with blue trousers. He has these big boots on his foot which again seemed expensive and his personality was way too intimidating. Anyone can sense his intellect from his body language. Perhaps, he was the first man in my work life whom I looked upon to become someday like him. Later, I checked out his LinkedIn profile to find out that he was from the Indian School of Business. I was in awe and realised that I certainly was not idolising a wrong man.

It started getting more cold as we entered January. Those were the days when I would be just finishing the tasks without even getting the time to understand what I was actually doing. Strange, right? But yes, this is how this supply chain project was taking a toll over me. I would consume some 5 to 6 cups of coffee within the day since I never had the habit of working this long on system.

I kept on filling in those check points till late January and started interacting with the people outside my department too. It was going pretty well with Vikas too since he would ask me to stay aligned with Tushar and the project and he himself would take care of the other planning tasks. I would never dare peeping at his tasks. To be honest, they looked dangerous from outside. He managed 2-3 people under him and would incessantly call them to update something. I would barely realise the jist of his conversation. Those 2-3 people were in the same team but I hardly interacted with them as this project was really overwhelming my entire day.

With January finishing, I was given tiny opportunities under my belt as well. I was terrible at Microsoft Excel in those days and had to struggle with tasks of 3-4 hours for some 2 days. The Head would peep in sometimes and ask me if I am getting aligned with my responsibilities. We would least interact those days. All the major discussions would be between him & vikas only. The funny part was, I had no official manager in my team. Vikas would report to the Head itself while I would report to someone who has least to do with my work. I thought it to be advantageous but I really missed the void of a manager.

By February, I was getting pretty comfortable with the project. I was understanding the gist of supply chain now. Atleast, I thought so. Till march, all I did was sit with Tushar & his team for hours and hours and hours. He would be irritated at times as I was not so professional, would address him Sir which he never liked and ask some really silly questions like a college student.

The Covid Wave

When we passed the first quarter of 2021, the second wave of covid created havoc. People were massively dying, the streets of Indore were empty as if no human life existed. I was both startled and shocked to see humanity dying. We were working from home but I was scared about my family. So I took the permission from my Head and flew back home.

The work from home had started and so were my good days, at least I anticipated it to be. But things were not as they seemed to be! In fact, it was the toughest patch of my work-life. Anyday, anytime be it my sleeping hour or the time I am having lunch, my phone would ring up. Sometimes it would be a purchase manager shouting after me and pinpointing my own work, sometimes it would be someone senior from my team asking for any particular report immediately. I would freak out and skip my lunch sometimes.

Thankfully, it didn't last and with half a year almost passed, we were back in the den. Homesickness happened for the first week but it got better. Eventually I started going out with some good friends I made there but real challenges were about to start.

CHAPTER TWO

THE IDEAL MANAGER

It was almost 8 months now in the organization. Till date, I wasn't allotted any immediate manager. On papers, I would report to a person who was not just super senior in the organisation but also had least to do with my work. Can you imagine me interacting with him, once in a blue moon, just to get my leaves approved before the month ending?

Now this 'No manager' was as much a bane for me as it sounded a boon. For any flaws in the system, I was being questioned directly by the higher authorities. The Head would call me now and then and when you directly work with a head, there are no 'No' options. You always have to be ready with the stance of 'Yes boss!' With time, it was tormenting me. At times, I would stay up late evenings, check on even the things a senior person must be assigned to, hold up responsibilities like which I barely had experience in and what not! Not to forget, I was still a fresher with a nominal salary but unlucky enough to work like a manager.

My stress levels were rising high with time and so was the amount of caffeine in my blood. And then one day, an email popped up! Everyone came and congratulated me. I, still nonplussed with the flows of these felicitations, checked on my mails!

The mail read:

Aman Verma has been assigned to the planning department as the Lead. From now on, Vikas and Akshay will report to him...

Hurrah was my instant reaction. No more managerial responsibilities, no more answerable I had to be to anyone. I felt like a free bird now. And why won't I be? I do not need to interact with the Head again and again.

Next day, Aman Verma called me at his place. I nonchalantly took my diary, a pen and my laptop to his cabin. As I reached there, he was going through some reports on his laptop. Lean, slender body with old fashioned glasses and thin hair decently combed, he looked like a typical 40 aged guy. One notable thing I noticed about him was his decency. He looked like the calmest person in that office. But I do not want to judge him in a nice way in the first meeting itself. I wanted to beware since he was going to be my manager from now on and it was corporate life. Although I believe in being human towards my co-workers, at the same time, I don't want to get backstabbed by anyone there. So, I chose to remain neutral with everyone.

Next, he welcomed me with a very cold attitude. Honestly, it was not a very good first impression. I perceived him as a boring guy with whom I am going to face a generation gap issue. We continued to introduce ourselves and then he asked me to explain all what we have been doing here. I started off and for the next 20 minutes, I didn't stop.

He looked serious and then stopped me there, "All this work, you do it yourself?" I wryly laughed, "Yes sir!" "This sounds way too much," "I know sir." After a long discussion, our conversation ended with a slight line of tension rising on his head. He looked a bit tense and I perceived that it's not going to be easy for him.

Since we were temporarily shifted to a new place, my seat was not fixed, and I would sit far away from him. I was with the thought that working in his cabin will refrain me from taking breaks, crack a joke or have fun which I usually do at my workplace. So, it became a daily fashion for me to greet him in the morning, discuss with him about the day's target and then wave him off by telling him that I will come to him in case I need him. But amidst that work, he'll definitely find me and run directly to me to share the updates or sometimes to take care of the uninvited problems which was the common thing at our workplace. His interruptions would often be misjudged by me. It often dragged me to conceive of him as a very irritating manager and I would ask my colleague to watch out for him in case he came here looking after me.

It was twenty days down the line, and it was all going in the same fashion. Same work style, same judgement and his same struggle for finding me. But one day, everything changed. I had committed a sort of blunder in one of my deliverables whose deadline was already crossed, and it was to be finished somehow by the end of the day. Me and Vikas, sitting there stressed out, calculated that it would take at least 5-6 hours to finish this.

It was some 2 in the noon with the scorching heat of September with AC not delivering it is best. We ran to Aman sir and informed him that how we were stuck, and it would take time to finish this activity. As anticipated, I knew that he wouldn't help much as it was not his duty to work on our deliverables and also he was in a senior position. It was a common fashion at that position to get the work finished by people at our level. But deep down I wanted him to support us in any way he could.

It was 5 by now and me & Vikas were still struggling with the jiggles of the situation. Bus timings were 5:30 and we dreaded we won't be able to finish by then. Vikas casually cracked a joke, "Aman ji how about you staying late with us and dropping us home by your car?" I giggled on this as he would be feeling troubled waiting for us beyond 5.30. To my surprise, he said he was okay with it.

Honestly, I didn't see this coming. People at his level, at least from my small experience, usually don't agree with his juniors. But he did. Although the next moment became a turn off when he said, "Try wrapping up quickly!" I was once again shattered as it seemed like a formality from him. I anticipated that he won't wait much and then me & Vikas would struggle through the late night bus.

Almost a 45-minute stretch was over, and our boss still chose to stand along our side. We three went for a quick coffee break and once again he said, "Can we wrap it quickly now? " Although, there was another 15-minute activity left but it agonised me as to why he was again and again asking us to hurry up. But then he added, "My eyesight doesn't support driving in the dark. Although, I'll manage, " saying this, he sipped his coffee. I was impressed both by his honesty & innocence. Next, we wrapped up the task and headed up for our homes in his car.

It was raining heavily outside. The wipers were cleaning off the water with high frequency and the wind seemed to be flowing with a decent velocity making it look like a blessed Friday setup.

Aman sir was driving while Vikas was accompanying him in the first seat while I rested myself silently on the backseat. Just then the silence broke up when I saw a completely different mode of Aman sir. He said it mischievously, "Yes, Akshay? Shall we stop here for something?" I looked outside and grinned with innocence as it was a Beer shop. "No, sir. I don't drink!" I said. "Don't be shy infront of me. You must be partying at weekends," he said again mischievously.

To be honest, I was comforted seeing this side of him. He was not that *khadoos* manager which I anticipated him to be earlier. As I really was a teetotaller, we headed and discussed more about our belongings. And this is when another green flag came into the picture. When I shared about my hometown, he surprisingly told me that he belonged to the same area and that we happened to be neighbours. Now, nothing could be more comforting than this and I felt closer to my manager.

He dropped us home and unlike other managers, he didn't drop us on the roundabouts or nearest auto stand but right outside our homes. I was honestly impressed by his gesture as my street was completely diverted from his route and I gave him the option to drop me off on the nearest square but it seemed like he hadn't forgotten the courtesy which although wasn't tough to learn but had become quite uncommon these days.

That evening everything changed. I no more looked upon my manager as a boss but chose to trust him like a friend. Our companionship started growing more with time. I started sitting more often with him now and with time, he was leaving no stone to show his great character.

Sometimes, he would ask for my monthly feedback which would surprise me like anything as it was not a common practice there to take feedback from their juniors. Sometimes, he would fight other managers to not consume my time so that I could focus on my work alone. I remember an incident of me getting sick so much that I couldn't go to my office for days and when I called him to inform that I'll be back soon, he instead of pushing me to come soon, asked me to relax and take my time. He even asked me to call him anytime for his assistance.

Things were going so smooth with him that I was once again falling in love with my job. He was backing me now and then, asking me to come up with my ideas and methodologies in my work style. And this was the first time, someone was understanding my true potential and asking me to think out of box, all because I had the capability to do so.

Within two months he has gotten very comfortable with our assigned work. He was not just handling well but guiding us to improve our methodologies which can make our lives easier. He wouldn't promote toxic culture even. He would often ask me to finish my work in a few hours and focus on bringing innovation for the rest of the time. I felt like a free bird that way and it was nothing lesser than a blessing to work under a manager like him.

CHAPTER THREE

Upper Circuit?

With my new manager coming into the picture, our working style has changed for the better. Our department was finally changing gears and we were finally working in a systematic way. Every character had a fixed role, every guy had a backup and most of the things were automated. Reports were getting minimised while automation was getting introduced in most of the methodologies. The activity which used to eat an hour usually was now a cake walk of barely 15 minutes.

I was finally shifting my focus to other areas of planning as well and was understanding the supply chain like I never did before. In short, I was having a good time with my work. And all thanks to my new manager who was managing the entire department pretty well.

Now I was no longer a trainee but officially a deputy manager who was not responsible or authorised just because of his title but also for the knowledge he held. People would respect me more and come up with their doubts and questions to me with a hope. I loved the hope they came up with and I would barely disappoint them since planning was comfortably coming under my control now. I could now answer most of the queries without checking my system and sometimes, I would quickly do the back calculations just in my mind and solve people's queries.

Things were going pretty smooth now and finally in the month of December, I was chosen the EMPLOYEE OF THE MONTH for my contribution as a demand planner to the team. That month, we introduced some 2-3 new methodologies and added to our improvements. Also, I was exploring supply chain beyond my work life as well.

From a motivation through a friend, I started writing about supply chain over linkedin as well. It was fun to prepare an article about your job work and it felt really good when some unknown people over the platform would jump in my DMs to thank me for sharing my insights about my supply chain.

I was totally loving this LinkedIn popularity so much that my curiosity made me drive to discuss things beyond our work with Aman sir as well. I thought he may consider it as a waste of time but he himself was so keen to share his knowledge that we would often have such discussions, sometimes in bus or sometimes during lunch discussion. I forgot to mention that our bond was growing so well that we would always have lunch together.

I remember an incident where I was working in his cabin. Just then, one of my good friends, Sarthak, messaged me that he has some free time and whether I would be okay doing a small bunk and going outside. It was a huge dilemma. In front of me was Aman sir who had just called me to finish some urgent work and on the other side, it was Sarthak who gave me a good opportunity to bunk the work.

I knew the criticality of the work he had given me just then as it was directly instructed by the Head. Otherwise he would have easily given me spare time which he normally used to. 15 minutes went by and the work was not progressing much. And there was a bombardment of messages from Sarthak that he was waiting. I couldn't stop myself and took a water bottle gesturing as if I would be back within a minute once the bottle was filled.

I ran downstairs along with him with a water bottle in my hand. We roamed outside the office for like 60 minutes and then he went back to his work. I was both embarrassed and scared that I didn't do the right thing and should have informed him at least. 60 minutes was a big leap for the urgency that task held. Shamelessly I went upstairs back to his work stead and what I saw embarrassed me to the core. He was simultaneously working on both the laptops, out of which one was mine. "I am so sorry, sir. Had an urgent call!" saying this, I started working and prepared the file as soon as I could have. He didn't utter a word and was as calm as I left him.

"Did you hear some scolding?" a text popped up from Sarthak later when I reached back. "Strangely, no!" I texted back while he was surprised. "Akshayy, your manager is the best. Don't ever do this to him again". He was right and from then, I never ditched him again.

The new year gave us new hopes and new beginnings. I anticipated to work more and grow in this organisation. Covid hit once and amidst this 3rd wave, we were asked to work from home. For the next three weeks, I isolated myself because both my roommates were covid positive one after another and somehow, I was saving myself from the infection.

Amidst this work from home sessions, I once again chose to grow myself. I would read more supply chain blogs, share my knowledge over LinkedIn, talk to more supply chain professionals and what not. I remember one incident where a supply chain lady appreciated my work and even asked me to mail my blogs to her. I was enjoying all such stuff and to ease my life at work, I did one certification program too which I shared with Aman sir and he undoubtedly commanded me to do the same.

My time was going pretty good. I remember one morning, waking up to my HR call. I was surprised as she barely calls me that time of the day. "Akshay, please join the meeting," she said and hung up. I joined up and there were top management professionals of the organisation. Half sleepy, I anticipated that this was some award ceremony and I guess, I was nominated for the same. Minutes later, I was felicitated with the award, and I couldn't be happy more. It was one of the highest awards in the forum and I was the bearer of it. I celebrated that moment and thanked Aman sir as well for being a part of my success journey.

Some 20 days were well spent and now that my roommates were safe along with the settlement of covid wave, I was joining the office from the next day.

CHAPTER FOUR

CHANGING SCENARIOS

Covid third wave has gone in a jiffy thankfully and my two roommates were recovered as well. I returned back to the office after some 20 days. To be honest, it did not feel the same way as it was in the past few months. I don't know why but I had this bad vibe drifting towards me from all directions. I was receiving a lot of glares from my colleagues as if I was on some 20 days' vacation and that I should feel guilty about this. Although, I didn't give a thing or two about their thoughts and continued focusing on my work which strangely I couldn't. Maybe, I had made myself too much comforted amid this WFH life or maybe I wanted a few more challenges now.

Same office, same repetitive issues, same complaints from the Head and like every time, no handmade prepared tea for us. I hate machine made teas & coffees. It was a different feeling. I was seeking bad in everything. What was retaining me was just my work and my manager, Aman Verma. I believed my work was pretty good and it was adding a lot of value to my resume. Apart from my manager, there was one more person who I thought backs me a lot of the time. She was the HR to our supply chain unit.

Everytime I have gone carrying complaints from my office, I haven't come back disappointed from her office. The least a person can do for you is to listen to your rants and she was perfect in that. No matter if the problem was solved or not, she would make sure to pave me the path I could go with. Apart from this, she was also a good friend whom I can approach any time in her office.

It was 15th of Feb. I had gone for just one day in the office post my 20 days quarantine and I again took a day off. No, there was not a proper pretentious reason I could say to my manager, so I said that I am not well. Honestly, I was having this anxiety of why I was actually serving in this organisation with a mediocre pay with a whopping number of working hours. I felt depressed earlier too about my lifestyle and work, thanks to my IT friends who have perks like Infinite leaves, Permanent WFH, double pay than mine, etc. I too wanted to have such perks but maybe I was not smart enough to fetch such jobs? I took this leave in a jiffy but never thought that one day this leave would change my entire career.

Next day when I arrived at the office, I dreaded that I would hear a lot of scolding. I didn't pick up the Head's call a day before and it would be the last thing anyone in the entire office could do. And Aman sir, you know? You can never understand from his face what's really going on in his mind, and he would barely scold me. Owing to all these situations I anticipated only fear and vowed that I would not take leaves at least for a month now.

But something was really not right that day. Aman sir gave some not so good hints like he asked me to document everything I had in my work profile and when asked what the need was to do so, he gave me a very lame reason. *Were they planning to prepare my backup?* I thought but then calmed myself and prepared to focus on my job. Interrogative questions from seniors like if I am too stressed or if I am married and carry too much responsibility in life, added more to my suspicions. My suspicions turned into 100% beliefs when I received a text from my HR, 'We need to talk'. Be it your girlfriend in personal life or an HR in your professional life, this sentence is both ways a sign of danger.

After my lunch, I wrapped up my work and headed to the admin building, the HRs place. Another thing added to my suspicions when Aman sir didn't question my visit to HR. He didn't ask a thing and asked me to go. When I reached the office, she was right there at her workstead, busy with some chores. She looked busy but still asked me to sit there and wait for her. Her body language didn't look different so I can finally have a sigh of relief that nothing much has happened.

Some ten minutes later, she was done with her chores, wrapped her documents and took her eye finally from the screen. "So, Akshay.. not interested in continuing your job here?" her question came as a surprise to me. I was surprised to see her tone and her expressions. Also, I was a bit fumed up by her question. I always considered myself a good employee to my organisation and never thought of being interrogated like this. So, my ego popped out and with a tinge of sarcasm, I replied, "If I was not interested in doing this job, why would I be sitting here?" She saw me getting heated up and told me that lets come straight to the point.

"Where were you yesterday, Akshay?"

"Yesterday, I was on leave!"

"And I heard that your favourite Aman Verma gave you 20 days WFH as well?"

"Actually, both my roommates were covid positive. I guess you know that. Also, I wrote officially to him and attached both of their covid reports."

She saw that I was not really enjoying this conversation. So, she cut off the useless conversation and came straight to the point, "See, I was there yesterday at your office. Both your boss and especially the head thinks that you don't want to work here anymore!"

"I would definitely inform you if such were my intentions, and I don't really understand what's the problem if I did WFH? I suggest you have a conversation with my manager about it!"

Seemed like she didn't like my giving back her answers. Plant culture, you see?

"You think Aman backs you?" her tone sounded worse here, and I was honestly shattered for a minute. It felt as if I couldn't trust anyone here. I already lost the trust in my HR and now she made sure to hate my manager as well. And it was not her words, I was personally disappointed too that why Aman sir didn't talk to me directly? Why was this communication sent to me through her?

Till date, it was the worst day of my job. Within a day, I felt disrespected and lost my trust in HR and my manager. I was already depressed but this conversation added more to my misery as well. My thoughts of leaving this job gained a lot of momentum that day. *They don't trust you for WFH, they interrogate you for one leave, they have trust issues despite your good performance.* The list was endless.

Sarthak witnessed all of this and came running to me after what happened there. He was supportive enough to both console and beware of people there. What he said ensured me not to trust anyone in this office. Afterall, it was the appraisal month!

That evening when I got off my bus, I didn't head to my apartment directly. I had an ice cream alone on the streets of Indore and walked around thinking of those days when I joined this organisation and how these people who were sweetest to me were altogether changing their colours like chameleons. I guess I was finally having the taste of real corporate life and the fad that management showed me during my earlier reign didn't last anymore.

CHAPTER FIVE

APPRAISAL SEASON

The night was not a pretty one. Imagine dedicating yourself to an organisation, especially when you are just a fresher in corporate and then having the feeling of distrust. I was distressed for the entire night. The night before, even though I was not in the right mood, the fact that people backed me at the office, motivated me every morning. But a small conversation with my HR was enough to lose that final hope too. I was just an employee who could be replaceable any day, irrespective of my capabilities, my contributions, my emotions, etc. That was the first time I felt so much hatred towards the organisation and its people.

The next morning although it dawned bright and sunny I can still feel the dark clouds clogging inside my brain. For whom I was working? The minimal salary? The suspicions my favourites raised against me at the cost of my dedication. Should I really work here even for a single day? Thoughts ran like a bullet train inside the cores of cerebrum.

The last time I felt horrible in this organisation were the days of December when I started feeling low about my salary, my organisation, the perks, etc. But it was Aman sir who backed me like anything and ensured that such thoughts can be pushed aside for a while. And then the likes of January (the third covid wave era) stopped all my thoughts of moving from here. For I can manage both my life and work with ease. But, this was the second time in a row when the thoughts once again came out, this time with much more intensity.

I reached the office on time but didn't complain a single word to anyone because there was no one in the office whom I could trust. Aman sir, as usual, called me to his place and discussed the tasks for the day. My expressions sent him the message pretty well that I was not in the mood to joke. Probably, it was the first time he was seeing this side of mine. Earlier, irrespective of my mood, I would open in front of him like a friend. It could be anything from 'Sir, I don't feel like working today." to 'I don't want to do this useless work...' He would listen and console me.

But today was quite different between us two. I was not uttering a word except for the work we were doing. He clearly understood that message had been sent to me. To better the environment around us, he asked in a casual tone, "Why did the HR call you yesterday?" I paused for a second and with a no-expression face muttered, "Uhh..there is some cultural program. She called me to enquire if I want to participate." "That's it? Anything else?" "No." Awkward silence. He was trying to have a discussion here, but I couldn't let my ego off the moment.

The next few days went in a similar fashion. There were few conversations between the manager and his favourite reportee. The two talked only for official purposes. No lunch together, no tea breaks, no jokes and least interaction. I was avoiding the seat at his workplace too and would go only for discussions. Rest, I would finish at my workplace only. Appraisal month was the talk of the town and it further added to my stress since my ego was not letting me have a conversation with my manager who would ultimately be going to rate me.

Three days had passed since I interacted but that day when I came back to my apartment, I felt a different vibe. I didn't know why but I wanted to give another shot to this job, and I thought about not letting this appraisal thing go in a jiffy. Another thing I wanted to do was to sort things out with my manager because I was struggling being too formal with him. So, I decided to go with the basics first and rather than complaining, thought of taking his feedback first. For it can be possible that I might have committed some mistake which I should have accepted or maybe what HR conveyed didn't really happen in the way she narrated. This was corporate and not a single person can be trusted, so I thought of taking his feedback on paper this time.

9.45 AM, the clock showed. The room, full of supply chain guys, was as usual surrounded with the air of anxiety. Everybody wanted the best rating and so, were ready to do anything to prove their worth. Honestly, I was not a big fan of proving myself altogether in the end, during appraisal month. I always believe my work speaks a lot about me and so I didn't need to shout loudest in the room.

I was at Aman sir's workplace. The tension of air between us still hovered because I hadn't talked to him for the past 3 days except those formal discussions. But that day, I chose to break this silence and have the transparency of his thoughts.

"Sir, let's sit in the conference room once we're done with our tasks. I need to discuss something with you." I muttered, with my head intact and eyes full of questions.

This is what he was waiting for. "Yes, please. Let's do it at 10!" He affirmed.

Those fifteen minutes were the longest for I was not sure where I should start with him? Should I ask him what happened that day? Or shall I ask if there's something going in his mind and he's not willing to share? Finally, the waiting period of 15 minutes came to halt. He ushered me to the conference room and we two comforted ourselves there.

I don't want to repeat the same mistake I did previously in the conference room with HR. I carried both my pen & notebook this time. I wanted to make sure whatever is being spoken is jotted down well.

"So, sir.. before we start this conversation, I want you to give me feedback on my skills, my performance, my behaviour, etc." As expected, he gave 10/10 feedback to me. As per him, I was both analytical and agile. And this job demands a person like that. I further inquired about my appraisal, my performance reviews, my improvement areas, etc. He crystal clearly told me everything. Also, after the discussion, I realised that my HR manipulated the conversation which I had with her earlier. I was definitely annoyed by her. Our 20 minute conversation came to halt and we headed outside the cabin.

I dedicated the next 10 days preparing my case for a good appraisal. The organisation didn't have any automated coverage of tasks we did the entire day. We were expected to prepare our case on power point for the whole year and submit it through the portal. I used all the graphics, visuals and data to prepare my form and submitted a week later.

CHAPTER SIX

SEEDS WERE SOWN

My frustration levels were still on peak. Even though the relationship with my manager was once again back on track and my appraisal was submitted for ratings too, I couldn't breathe a sigh of relief.

My frustrations were rising so high that the only path to escape all of this were my friends, Sarthak & Vishwas. They were few of the sane people I had come across and would always help me better my mood. Whenever I would feel low, I would ask them to plan some outing, which can be a mood freshener and they would always show up.

I remember one of the weekends around the first week of March where we three of them planned to roam around. Right after the office on a friday, I went to their place to stay and have a boys night out. We roamed around the famous Chappan market of Indore, where we tried almost 10 to 15 different cuisines, laughed our heart out and like a typical engineer, judged many people out there, making them an object of laughing material for us. It was fun. I had totally forgotten the world inside VECV, for I was totally lost amidst this chaos of my bachelorette fun.

We came back that night very late to their apartment. The apartment was amidst the city life with a balcony where one can directly talk to stars. We had deep conversations about love, life and office. We slept on the mattress laid on the open verandah where a gush of chil wind from outside was caressing our bodies, which gradually made us fall asleep. That night, I slept like a carefree baby after a long time.

The night passed and so did the Friday happiness and subsequently the Saturday too. I was once again back to the mourning of Sunday evening. Sipping through the pomegranate juice, I realised how tough it would be to transit once again from my friend's world to office life. I felt as if something heavy was twanging in my stomach. Even the juice forbade going inside my oesophagus that evening.

We all have that Sunday anxiety dreading Monday morning but this was actually quite very different. I felt so depressed that night that I couldn't feel excited when my neighbour, Karishma di welcomed me for dinner with mouth watering *kadai paneer*. Trust me, I still felt like throwing out. The night passed with terror and like every day, I headed for the office.

It was the 7th of march. Right from 8AM, I couldn't just concentrate but also couldn't breathe properly. There was something wrong with the day or maybe that life. I could see that Aman sir was still not in office and it became quite evident once I received the message of him attending his daughter's parents meeting at school.

It was 9 in the morning. All the reports were released from my end but something was still not right. I did some chit chat over calls, called my mother, talked with everyone I could and then my nasty mind did something which finally raised up my adrenaline. I randomly messaged my cousin brother who was an ISB alumnus. *"Bhaiya, job chod ke CAT ki tayari karna.. sounds like a wise choice?"* "Yes, not bad!" came the reply. I shivered once again to write, *"1.5 saal ka experience hai bs mujhe.. Still wiser choice?"* "Yes, you can go for it!"

After this conversation got over, my heart felt lighter first and then heavy like a boulder. For a part of me knew that I was going for a 'Quit'. Yes, I was quitting. I didn't want to haste so with a raised heartbeat, waited for Aman sir to come back. He came back in the second half and after a very boring report, took me to lunch. I was still quite nauseating so I fed myself with just radish and rice followed by a glass of lassi. Obviously, it wasn't the right time for that discussion so I postponed it for the evening.

We came back to our desks and continued with our work. Call it destiny ringing some bells for me, all the useless work was on my head that day and it was motivating me more to leave that job. It felt as if everything was conspiring to make me quit that job. By the time it was 4 in the evening, my head called me to ask about the whereabouts of pricing in the sales team. Another out of the box task, I mean never in my job of 18 months, I went into the pricing thing and he was enforcing something like that at this point of time. Strange!

By 5.10, I planned to ask Aman sir if he would drop me home that day since that would be the best time to discuss my plans with him. But another unusual thing happened when he decided to stay after 5.30 that day and our journey of my resignation discussion could never take place. As he was quite occupied, I decided to board my bus on regular time and thought of delaying this conversation until the next day.

It was 6.39 in the evening. The dusk had set in and I had just entered my apartment. Although, it had always been my happy place but that day it gave me a different kind of horrifying vibes. The book collection which always supported me in my worst time seemed to be withered and helpless. The curtains looked helpless, the window view gave no moral support, the aesthetics remained silent and the list was endless. I had decorated each and every corner of my room with my own bare hands and considered each of those to be my friends.

But on this day, they all looked helpless. They all were mourning my pain and grief. Or maybe they had sensed that I was about to leave them all and they were all too upset to show any vibes in the room? Dusk had started setting in and the outside natural light had bid off a bye. I didn't have the energy to turn on the room lights for I somehow wanted to remain in the darkness adding more to my melancholy.

With uniform on, I was lying on the bed grieving about the episodes of this morning. Unlike everyday routine, I had forgotten to bathe even, retaining every bit of negative energy I inculcated from the office that day. Grieving and overthinking, I went talking to myself about my resignation. "Shall I discuss with Aman sir, first?" "Akshay, he's always backed you." "Shall we text him?" "Let's talk to him tomorrow morning... no.. let's message him now"

And then suddenly, my phone squeaked in silence with a phone call. I stretched my hands to the sofa to pull my phone while lying on the bed. It was Aman sir. My heart skipped the beat. "Is it the time? Shall I talk to him right?" Phone bell continued ringing loudly, alarming me as if it was an important moment of my life. I swiped up to pick the call and before I could say anything, the call started like owning the one way ticket to this conversation.

"Akshay, listen there is an emergency and we need to close off. Can you please login into your system and do the needful?" His words added more to my ever ending and excruciating pain. I would have blasted him with my words.

"Sorry sir, I am not in a condition right now, please try to understand!"

He still continued to plead.

"Sir, but.." "Akshay yaar...Samjha kar na... directors are all after us. Please do it. Take your time, do it around 8. Okay? Bye!" The call was disconnected.

Despondent and exasperated, I threw off my phone because my rage was uncontrollable now. The only hope of Aman sir had faded too. It was a "Go hard or Go home" situation for me now. I chose the former.

Wiping off my tears, I got off from my lying state. I picked up my phone and typed a long message to Aman sir. With quivering fingers and firm mind, I wrote,

"Sir, it's very tough to work in this environment. At times, I feel running out of energy. The expectations are too high, the resources way too less. This has become a daily fashion and I literally feel both demotivated and exhausted. I have tried reaching the higher management but I can't seek any support.

I am afraid sir if I can continue like this!"

And sent!

Post this hard decision, I climbed down my bed or maybe once again in the job hunt market. Although I had no hopes to work here anymore but was anticipating that the people would ask me to stay. The floor felt cold to my feet and the no sign of slippers was a clear message to me. Next few months are going to be exactly like this. I would be barefoot for a good amount of time but definitely I won't give up.

With one side my thoughts running, I finally decided to freshen up and relax. Looking straight into the mirror, with my sleeves rolled and my hairs tousled up, I can see those teary eyes now ready to fight. A lot can be seen beyond that mirror that day. My rage was clearly asking me to show all what you have for I had anticipated that this time it was not just going to be a cat fight but there would be battles everyday and someday I would lose too but the bigger goal was to win the war for I had strongly believed myself to be a warrior.

By 8PM, I had quite a few times checked my WhatsApp now. But there wasn't a single message from him. It was a bit of a shock for me as I thought he would definitely back me but then I thought that maybe he wanted to talk to me in person? But definitely a text message was expected from his side and his no reply definitely added to my disappointment.

By 8.30, I left both my room and my miseries to have dinner with my favourite Karishma didi. I didn't care about my job, about my manager, about the next day or about anything at that moment. All that I wanted was to spend my time with her because she always treated me like her son. I went ahead to her room and had my favourite *rajma chawal*. With all the love, she made me eat till my stomach was burst. *"Ab office mein sab theek hai beta?"* She nonchalantly asked.

"Ab sab theek rahega!" I smiled back and took another bite of rajma chawal.

CHAPTER SEVEN

Nehle pe Dehla

The next morning dawned with the chirping of birds and the sun rays peeping inside my room through the windows. The presence of sunlight and the playful activity of birds were the clear indication that I had missed my 7.15 AM bus to the office but the fact that I had slept till this hour of the morning were clear signs about the peaceful sleep I had last night. I checked on my phone to find it was some 9 in the morning and the fact that there were neither any missed calls nor any mails had worried me a bit. To my surprise, Aman sir had yet not replied. Clearly, something was not right. But as I was already firm with my decision, I had decided to be in the footsteps of a famous movie released those days, Pushpa. *"Main jhukega ni Saala!"*

I still anticipated my team to message me first and asked about my whereabouts and if not, at least Aman sir had to talk to me on the message I sent him last evening. As a manager, it was his moral responsibility to talk about my pain, provided he wanted to back me. In the next half hour, I did all the morning chores and walked towards Karishma di's house to have breakfast. With a laptop and charger in my hand, she mockingly asked, *"bachcha aaj bhi WFH le Liya? Chal yahi se kaam Karle"*

I was done with my breakfast. Didi offered me *chaach* and then mockingly asked me if I was not having work today since I looked too ideal. I smiled and asked if she had some *laddoos* since my mouth was craving for some sweets. She didn't have any in her house, so I immediately went out to a sweet shop to get 500 gms of Besan ladoo.

While the laddoos were being packed, I received a phone call. It was from Richa. Richa was a recruiter from a sports e-commerce firm and had taken my interview earlier for the role of Demand Planner. She called to ask for my confirmation if I would be okay to join their company from the Bangalore office at said amount. Now, this was not something exciting for me since both the location and especially money were too mediocre for me. I still said Yes and hung up the call. Back of my mind, this Richa was a token of belief I hold in the market so I didn't want her to go.

At 11 AM, I reached di's house to greet her with ladoo. After having a good laughter session, I casually opened my laptop to check if there were any mails. It was a big blow over my face. I felt as if someone had stabbed me right on my face. Not Aman sir but it was a mail from the Head itself.

Subject: *Vishwas to be handed over to the Planning Department.*

To: *Aman Verma; Vikas; Vishwas; Akshay Pratap Singh*
Team Planning,
I am giving Vishwas to the Planning department under Aman for next two months. He would learn under you all and would be assessed by me weekly.
Thanks
Sachin Singhania
Head

Vishwas was my junior in the office. Like me, he had joined the company as a GET from my junior batch. He didn't hold any projects till then but dreading my exit, the management handed him over to our team, preparing him to be my replacement. To be honest, I was both shocked and dejected. I couldn't feel my body over the couch. Everything that surfaced was turning cold. I could feel the shivers running through my body. I was so disappointed that the next moment, I directly opened the resignation window in the laptop and started filling the form. I was shivering, raging, running so high on energy that I could have broken down those keys I was typing my resignation with. Everything was done except the final 'submit' button.

But my senses came back to reality and asked me to calm down. My inner voice clearly instructed me, "Not in a haste..please take your time, give one last thought and then do whatever you feel like... not in a haste!" I closed the window, shut down my laptop and ran in a haste towards my room. I asked didi to not prepare my lunch since laddoos were enough to energise me for the day. I promised her that I'll be back at dinner.

Running back, I reached my room, locked myself from inside, threw my laptop, phone, charger, keys, everything on the sofa and took a deep breath. It was hard to believe that those guys were so shallow.

I watched myself closely into the mirror and started talking to my reflection.

"See, I have always respected you and won't ever let you down ever. Today what happened has definitely hurt you to the core. So listen to me carefully. It's 1 in the noon.. you have a full day. I promise I'll help you make the decision before you go to the office tomorrow!"

Simultaneously my other side questioned, "Why don't you want me to resign right now when everything is so clear?"

"Because someday when you'd look back to this day, you should feel the pride in yourself not the regret. It should be a memorable day of your life."

I sighed a deep breath, and asked myself to calm down. Next, I prepared a timetable of the next 8 hours in my mind. I ordered something for lunch and then went for a sound sleep as if nothing had really happened. I knew last night's sleep wasn't enough to quench my pain and that I needed more calmness before I made some big decision. I retired myself for a long afternoon nap.

By the time I woke up, it was 6 in the evening. The first thought that came to my mind was about putting down my papers. I was about to start my task only when my phone rang. It was Karishma di's. She wanted me to come to her house and assist her with cooking. I couldn't deny that she was more like my mom. I didn't want to make a decision in haste so thought of going to her first and then coming back and getting done with my decision.

It was more than a typical good vibes in her house. Sweet smell of *agarbatti*, holy bhajan songs, yellow lights everywhere while she dressed in yellow saree like *Sita Maa*. I was also feeling emotional for her since I didn't want to leave her.

When I asked her what she needed, she said that she just wanted me to sit there till dinner as she can have some gossip with me till cooking. It was very clear that she won't let me go then and I definitely can't delay more.

After some 15-20 minutes of gossip, I asked for a pen and paper and told her that I wanted to plan something on it. She gave her five year old daughter's bag and asked me to find something from it. I started rummaging through her bag only to find a few colourful erasers, four lined English register and some kids' pencils. Seems like all these decisions would be made by a kid in me, not an adult. I tore off a piece of paper from that notebook, took one pencil and started working.

I got myself locked again and asked didi that I just had to prepare for some presentation I had in the office the next day and that I would just be back in 20 minutes. Once again, deep breaths were taken and with a calm mind, I proceeded. Plans for the next year, CAT options, all the worst apprehensions, etc. were being jotted and analysed. A fine comparison was done too with my current situation and after going through every buts and ifs, it was clear that resigning overpowered everything.

That was it! I was resigning. I had a smile on my face but my eyes were definitely watery. I folded that paper, put it inside my pocket and kept the pencil back inside the bag.

"*Hogya kaam beta?*" She asked while kneading flour for chapatis. I nodded my head since I was not in a mode to speak. In fact, I realised how much I would miss my second mother who has always supported me in my worst times.

"*Kya khaayega mera beta?*"

"*Kuch bhi bana do maa!*" I hugged her tight.

While the food was being prepared, I was standing outside on the balcony with thoughts running one after another. I was in an emotional state I had never been during my entire stint at this firm. I was definitely feeling bad about how I was being treated and how I never wanted to leave this city in such a fashion.

With the decision being made in my mind, my entire life at this firm started playing in front of my eyes in a very fast-paced manner. How I joined this firm two years ago, how I faced numerous challenges, how I never chose to give up and continued thriving no matter what challenge came in the way. It was a rollercoaster ride which gave me so many memories to look back and not to forgot, made me in a position from where I could take this tough decision.

After having dinner with di, I went for a long walk with her and her husband. Like everyday, we were having this funny conversation about the office, her neighbours etc.

Around some time, I came back to my room and it was some 11 in the night. I started preparing for the next day as usual. I ironed my dress, polished my shoes, chopped off some fruits to carry them to the office and then went upstairs inside my room. The only activity was left brushing my teeth before bed. I thought of doing so but the human inside me melted finally and standing in front of the mirror, I bursted into tears like anything. With tears rolling down my cheeks, I would brush one side of the mouth, spit off in the sink, brush the other side and cry.

The clock showed 11.55 in the night now. I wiped off my tears now and opened the resignation window in my system. I wrote,

"Thanks team for all the support. I hereby confirm my resignation from the post of Deputy Manager!"

And SENT!

CHAPTER EIGHT

9TH MARCH, 2022

That day, morning in Indore was altogether different. What happened in the past 40 hours was still indigestible to me. But one thing was sure, I was pumped up like anything. I literally felt as if instead of office, some battlefield awaited me. More than the fear of my future in the next upcoming months, I was more excited to fight and win from here.

Even after I was done bathing, I was incessantly gibbering to calm down my anxiety. While buttoning my shirt in front of the dressing table, I was constantly mumbling, "Don't you give up from here please," and then wrapping up all my morning chores, went on to board my bus like everyday. I had made up my mind that I'll be as Akshay as I was in the past 18 months during my stint and would continue to be sincere to the management as long as things don't go south.

My bus would usually reach the main plant around 7.45 in the morning and from there, another bus would be there to drop me to the warehouse, where I actually seated. When I reached the main plant, I trotted towards *Hanuman mandir* and nonchalantly thanked him for helping me make this decision and then anxiously started walking towards my bus.

By 7.50, every guy from the warehouse would be on the bus. That day too, when I stepped inside, it was fully packed and there at the end, I could see Aman sir sitting alone on a window seat. To be honest, I couldn't feel the guts to make eye contact with him and seeing his expressions, I felt bad for he was the saviour in my job who wouldn't just back me every day but would also be my best friend. Before taking this step, I wanted to discuss with him but the universe conspired something else.

In the next 5 minutes, we're at the warehouse. Unlike every day, it was a different day. No bad trips, no rants, no chit chats. I went to my seat and immediately opened my system to log in. Inside, it was hurting me so much but I had apprehended that coming days would pass in this fashion only. Usually, early morning hours would start with the conversation between me and Aman sir but that day we didn't exchange even a word till 10. I was busy finishing my tasks, talking to my teammates about the previous day's issues, etc. My friend Sarthak, who would sit beside me, was surprised too. He was closely observing my odd behaviour but didn't say anything. Although, a day later I informed him about my resignation.

Around 10.15 AM while I was busy preparing a report, I heard my name from behind. It was Aman sir asking me for a discussion inside the conference room. I wrapped up my things and headed for it.

The room was too warm to tolerate the heat. Maybe, it was because of the discussion we were heading towards. I comfortably seated and lowered down the AC to 16 degree Celsius. I wanted to ensure we both came out without carrying any heat within.

"Akshay Pratap Singh, Monday tak toh sab theek tha. Kal kya hua achanak?" He started the question with a faint

smile. I smiled back. It was my first expression of the morning.

"Kaha theek tha sir? I even texted you.."

"Okay, what problems do you exactly face here?" He came directly to the point.

"I have already informed you umpteen times sir. I am tired now. No work balance, no boundaries, no respect. They pay me in peanuts and expect me to mine gold. I am literally tired. And look at your boss and his behavior. Few weeks back, I took WFH for sometimes and everyone raised an eye on me. This shows the trust. I literally feel scared taking even a day off here. I guess, few things can't be changed, so I guess I had to change myself." I vented out in one breath.

He has perceived that he won't be able to stop me. And perhaps he saw this day coming. Unlike others, he didn't fake anything and asked me to at least give him proper feedback. I made him jot down all the points I can and he, without any objection, wrote all. Such a professional guy he was and deep down, I did want to work along with him more but unfortunately cannot.

We came out of the conference room with a faint smile on our faces. Nevertheless, no one on the floor knew what was going on in the planning department. No one knew about my resignation except our Head. And he was annoyed as hell. He neither wanted to retain me nor wanted to talk about it. He has already instructed Aman sir to prepare Vishwas for my replacement.

The entire noon went with my thoughts hovering around. Good decision or bad decision? I was constantly being attacked by my thoughts. Thankfully, I didn't inform anyone otherwise people would have made sure to make me believe it as a bad decision. Post lunch, I saw HR had arrived at my workplace. I anticipated she might talk to me but ego was so much in the air. Likewise my head, she too chose to ignore me and didn't even consider talking to me.

I was so happy that I chose not to work among such people and that struggling would be a better option than constantly pleasing such peers. Worst she did was that she secretly informed Sarthak even before I informed him. He didn't talk to me for some time since as a friend he expected that I should have informed him. Things were going south for me just because I chose to resign. Besides all this melodrama, I was doing KT sessions with Vishwas alongside managing the daily chores too. It was getting so hectic.

The thoughts kept on pondering, giving me a sense of negativity and fear. The entire day passed like this.

It was 5 now and to my fortune, I received a call from an unknown number,

"Am I talking to Akshay?" A high pitched voice heard from the other end.

"Yeah, who's this?" I replied promptly.

"Akshay, this is Stefi from CG Consultancy and we have shortlisted your profile for Supply Chain Consultant role. Would you be interested?"

I couldn't believe my ears. Was it happening this quick?

"Yes, stefi. I would be interested. Please go ahead!" I replied without showing much ecstasy. She scheduled an interview call for the next day and I, beating my pumped fist in the air, celebrated. "We are not backing off. Indeed, God is with us!"

CHAPTER NINE

RANMBHOOMI

Days of struggle have started. I didn't have time to spare even for a minute. I would continue applying on job portals and side by side, would ask my friends to refer me to their companies. Since CG has already given me an interview call, I had to look into the preparation of the same as well. I was so bombarded with everything that I would sleep less in the night, wake up fresh in the morning to surf naukris even on commode, study something from YouTube or udemy during bus ride to office and on reaching office, immediately unpack myself to jot everything down in my diary.

The tasks would be like : follow up with this referral, interview preparation notes, KT to Vishwas, etc. First half would usually be spent with Vishwas explaining everything, second half would usually be dedicated to some work escalations and the rest would be dedicated to impressing the recruiters on LinkedIn. Things were getting hectic while challenges continued to grow.

Even if I would get a call for an interview, one of the major challenges was to settle my interview slot amidst my office hours. I wasn't allowed to take leave in notice period, 6.30 PM would be too late for recruiters while on weekends, no interviewers were available. To settle down this challenge, I would stay in the office till 7 in the evening so as to finish my interview calls in the office conference room itself.

I finally gave the interview to CG next week. They seemed to be quite impressed by my skills and I anticipated to receive the offer soon. I finally felt some relief and another good news was that my current HR wanted to negotiate and retain me i.e. I was given the choice to change my location and can even demand for a better pay. Though I was not interested, I agreed since I wanted to hold everything I can which can help me make the decision lately.

Amidst all this, I also wanted to spend some time with my friends, who used to live amidst a city life. On weekends, I would plan a stay at their apartment only. We would binge watch movies, read books and plan some kind of sports together. I remember buying expensive shoes in a mall one Saturday for I wanted to gift myself something. Vishwas would lent me some really different books to read. I remember him offering a book on Mumbai life and how it talked about the struggles of Mumbai from a middle class person perspective in the time when it was Bombay. Few of the weekends would pass like this, especially when I would feel a burnout amidst my preparation journey.

It was the second week of my notice period somewhere around 16th march when Aman sir asked me to have a discussion with the HR. I was called in the morning that day but owing to her busy schedule, HR kept on postponing the meeting. I had lunch there itself with Aman sir but the time of meeting was still on hold.

Finally we reached there around 4.30 in the evening but the HR Head still seemed to be busy. While we waited outside, I was thinking of negotiating with them for some hike and definitely about the options in Gurgaon. We were waiting outside only when my phone received a notification. It was CG's. My adrenaline rushed because I knew it would definitely be the result of my interview. As I opened to check my mail , it was a congratulatory mail. I was selected. I was on cloud nine since I didn't anticipate that I would fetch an offer in the first week of my notice period itself. Either I was too talented or my stars were in the right direction. I was pumping up my chest in imagination. First good offer was on the table.

The euphoria was interrupted when finally the HR got the chance to call us inside. I had already informed her last night that I would be interested in discussing the Gurgaon option. But this all of a sudden CG option changed the entire story. The meeting started and I kept on saying NO to everything my HR offered. It was funny in some way. Aman sir might be laughing too inside his head as the HR Head made that poker face on hearing my consecutive NOs.

"But you said, you wanted to discuss those Gurgaon options?" HR asked.

"Umm sorry, I now have another offer from Gurgaon!" Poker faces followed. Honestly, I might have annoyed them but I guess they deserved that.

Aman sir and I came out of the office in about thirty minutes. He laughed about the discussion and taunted me, *"Tu jaake hi maanega na?"* I laughed hearing this. He gave a faint smile too. We wished each other Happy Holi and by evening I flew to my hometown just for a 2 day trip since I couldn't afford any more leaves.

I had the plan to discuss my resignation with my father but guess what? They were too busy with festivals and house chores. Sadly, I had to fly back again to Indore without having any sort of conversation with my family. A notable thing happened on the way. I got an unknown call from a medico startup. They wanted to interview me for a business specialist role. Thanks to my junior who referred me here and the HR liked my resume. This was going to be challenging since this role needed the coding background.

My routine was becoming more and more hectic. I was following coding before and after office since the interview was scheduled in a week and it was becoming a very tough task. Apart from that, negotiations with both Richa and Stefi were going for compensation in E-commerce & CG respectively. Richa was not offering me good compensation while Stefi was taking time to help me know if I could get a better location. Stefi had offered me Chennai initially and I couldn't go to the southern part of India and now she wasn't replying for a location change. I wasn't satisfied with either of the offers because I didn't want to compromise on anything.

My coding marathon started. I seriously started watching coding lectures in the bus hours, would even compensate in the office hours sometimes and then take up with office work too. My interview for this medico startup was again on the weekdays at some odd hour. I didn't choose to stay in office till late evening hours, rather ran during the office hours itself. Aman sir was supportive enough to look into my leaves.

The D-day came and medico's interview happened. I was asked some difficult questions which I couldn't answer. The other answers which I gave were half correct. Consequently after the interview, I was shattered. I knew I didn't stand a chance.

Richa continued calling me every single day and I continued asking her to come up with a better compensation and to even hold my joining for at least one month. She would agree to it and wait. Though this offer was not a delight to my heart. My anxiety levels were rising because Stefi from CG was neither giving any answer nor picking up my calls. She hasn't responded about my reallocation from Chennai to any north India location.

I was afraid then. Stefi's no response gave me an apprehension that she won't be changing my location. On the other hand, I had almost failed medico's interview too. I can feel myself soaring up inside negativity once again. My emotions were being tousled up every now and then.

I had everything to lose so I couldn't afford to give up. Even in the worst state of my mind, I can't give up. I continued fighting and randomly started asking for referrals from my friends. I asked referrals from my Bain & Co friend, my sister-in-law from Accenture, my cousin brother from Amazon, and my brother-in-law from PWC. I literally called everyone I knew, in that period. I didn't stop from clicking on the right profiles on the naukri portal. Additionally, I asked my seniors who were at very good positions in Big4 to help me get a job.

I got back to Chinmayee (the HR from medico) to check about my interview status. Although I was damn sure about my rejection, she said that she completely forgot to inform me. I am pushed for the next round. I couldn't believe it. For a moment, it felt as if I was injected in some oxygen to relive. I once again started to revise my coding concepts and prepared myself for the next round.

Within 3 days, the interview happened. The interviewer was very jolly this time. We talked about my current profile, my interests, IPL matches, etc. I also answered a lot of his questions. In short, it went very well. I was quite confident to nail it this time but 3 days later, an email popped up which apologised, for I was rejected.

Once again, I was back to zero. I continued running after Stefi. She wasn't responding yet. Richa didn't show any interest in better pay and there was no reply from any of the referrals I received. To be honest, I was shattered. My shoulders were drooped down and I couldn't understand why I wasn't getting any results. My situation was of a warrior in the battlefield, who was not only fighting alone but was also stabbed so many times that injury took all his energy.

I can't even think about giving up, after all I didn't have any options. I had made my mind programmed that giving up is not an option here and I have to keep on fighting anyhow. After the string of rejections, I was quite devastated.

But as they say, *Picture abhi baaki hai*. And one afternoon, the ray of hope seemed to be alive once again. I was sipping coffee on the terrace of my office along Sarthak while he was cracking some really poor jokes to somehow lighten my mood. Between those jokes, my phone rang with a very weird name shown by the truecaller. I picked up and a professional female voice spoke. After confirming my name and verifying my profile on naukri portal, she asked a question(which had a very obvious answer to it),

"Anyhow, have you worked on demand planning and forecasting, Akshay?"

I smirked as it was my daily routine. I replied, "Yes of course. That's a part of my job here."

"Great. Shall we schedule an interview call for you?" She asked.

I was not very delighted initially as I haven't heard the name of this company before. It was some AI company which provided analytics solutions. But what she offered me next brought a big smile on my face. She offered me much more than what all other recruiters were willing to offer and along with that, a WFH choice and theGurgaon location. I instantly realised that this was something we can't let go. I got so desperate that when she asked me whether I would be okay for an interview for the next day or the next week, I immediately asked her to schedule it for the next day.

The injured fighter has finally got some healing to once again roar back in the battlefield. For the next few days, I continued doing all the homework and got myself prepared. Once again, I persuaded Aman sir to give me some incentive for leaving office before time and he once again agreed. Such a supportive person he was.

The interview evening finally came and I didn't let any ball go out of my control. I answered every question pretty well and received a compliment from the interviewer. He was so impressed that in the interview itself, he confirmed me for the next round. I couldn't be happier. I hoped best for the next round. It was three days before the next round. And as they say, when you don't give up, everything starts getting in your favour. Next day, Stefi called me back and offered me the suitable location. Another call came from a research advisory company and they too scheduled an interview. Everything was going in my favour now.

Second round came for the same AI company. I was well prepared this time too but for the first half, it didn't go well. I screwed up a few of the questions so much that I started feeling amidst the interview itself that I have lost this opportunity. At least, the interviewer's expression said so. But next, the most important part of the interview came. It was some theory which I explained to him in such a good way that he seemed to be impressed. The final words in the interview sounded as if there were some hope. The interview came to an end and for the next few days, I was nervous if I would be able to make it or not.

A few days later, during the first week of April, I received a meeting invite for HR discussion. I was overjoyed that I cleared the second round too and it seemed that it was merely a game of formality now. We had a call in the evening and with some basic questions, she said "Welcome to our company!". I couldn't be happier. I wanted to dance like a maniac but didn't want to be a Mushfiqur Rahim who celebrated when 2 was needed from 3 and ended up losing. I calmed down and waited for the next few days for the official mail from them. Till then, fingers crossed.

CHAPTER TEN

FATEH

Light. Camera. Action! Yes this is how this day should be started with, for I felt more like a protagonist of some movie. A movie too good to be called a reality.

After fighting this whole battle of resignation, I had the feeling that I was winning it like a *Kshatriya* and I can't be proud of it anymore. My body language has become once again positive now not because of the results I was getting but because of the bravery & the courage I showed in the past few months. I was super proud of myself and this morning too, when I slipped in my uniform and looked into the mirror, I said to myself, "Great job. Let's be grounded and continue winning like this" I combed my hair, slipped in my shoes, wore my watch, locked my door and went ahead to catch my bus.

It was some 7 in the morning and apart from the Spring, there was definitely some magic in the air that day. Although this AI company, for which I gave an interview last week, was yet to release the offer, what I was more proud of was how I tackled all of this situation.

I reached the office and everything seems to be under control now. Stefi has agreed for the desired location, Richa has agreed to wait and I have almost pulled off an offer a day before for AI company and now the wait was for the official mail from them.

That morning, I was humming some Bollywood songs infront of Aman sir and side by side taking up some notes in my diary. It may sound weird but the bond between me & him has grown a lot I mean, more than the tension he had about my departure, he was happy about my rescue from this place. Like a true leader, he always wanted me to grow in my career. That morning, seeing me jolly, he could very well understand my expressions and started pulling my leg, *"Lagta hai bahutt offers aa rahe hai kisi pe?"* I laughed hard on this and then mocked around that he should resign too and move on with me. We laughed and our banters kept continuing.

Amidst that conversation only, my phone rang. Those days, my phone's ringtone either used to be good news or bad news. And every time it rang, my heartbeat would tousle. The true caller showed some unknown number and honestly I couldn't guess it either. I went outside the office and picked up the call.

"Hey Akshay. I am Sobit from the AI company!" It was a hoarse voice and he seemed to be some HR from the same company I was waiting for an offer from. We had a short call and he indicated that to continue the process, he expected a few documents from me. I already had those arranged and sent him immediately. There was no reply to my documents mail within the next few hours and I even thought that it would take him a few days to get back. To my surprise, I received his reply that day itself.

4PM it was when I was sipping coffees with my colleagues and sharing gossips. Amid all this, my phone vibrated. It was Sobit's mail which officially said I was being a part of their team and below attached were the three documents regarding the policies and compensation. I don't know what really happened but I felt like crying at that moment. And honestly, I couldn't bear a second standing and sipping coffee among my peers. I needed some time to settle myself. That feeling, those goosebumps, those emotions.. all of those were hard to take in.

I wanted to express myself. I left the coffee in between, packed my bag and left for my room. Once again, I asked Aman sir to give me some incentive in my leave card.

In the next half an hour, I could find myself standing in a cyber cafe, waiting to get my documents printed. The printout guy took a few minutes and handed me a hard copy of my offer letter. I paid him and started walking towards my room.

The sun was headed towards the west while I was headed to a completely new path. Holding that offer letter, I started strolling like a maniac with no idea about my surroundings. All my past struggles, all those teary nights, all those bad dreams were reflecting in a flash. I was crying damn hard while my tears flowed down my cheeks. To all those efforts, to all those courageous nights, it was worth it. And I.. I did it on my own. Surrounded by the crowd and walking on the same path I was running on from the past few months, I was crying the tears of joy. I kept on strolling, let my tears flow and clapped like a maniac for myself. I felt like Will Smith of 'The pursuit of Happyness' and actually felt 'this part of my life, this little part, is happiness!'

I continued crying, continued clapping and went ahead in the glory of the day.

I couldn't be more thankful to God and went to a nearby temple to greet him. The notable thing of the day was: there was no one with whom I could share my happiness because barely anyone knew about my resignation and perhaps I didn't want to share it either. I went for a long walk in the night and had a really good ice cream, celebrating my day with my very own company. That day when I went to my bed in the night, I realised how beautiful a peaceful sleep looks like.

CHAPTER ELEVEN

THE LAST DAY

The night of 19th may was the longest for me, for the next day I was officially going to be free from the shackles of my organisation. I always called that office a *chakravyuh*, a maze where it's not tough to make an entry but once you get in, you only come out either as a loser or as a dead person. But I somehow survived like a modern day *Abhimanyu*.

Jokes apart, I also carried the emotions with this organisation because it was my first job and also I found some good relationships through this organisation. I can't be thankful enough for this organisation. If it weren't for this organisation, I would have barely taken such risks in my life. Emotions were damn high and so was my insomnia for the night.

I barely slept the entire night and when I finally got some sleep, it was already the morning of the big day. 20th may, the day which would always be a testimony of my courage. I did it. Not only I got over a toxic job but also created a base for my career going ahead. In the past few months, without any family's or friends support, I quit a toxic job, applied for some 50 jobs, gave some 10 interviews and bagged 5 offers in a row. And this all happened going against my management, against some stupid advice while listening only to my heart. It wasn't an easy thing and if you ask me today to do this all over again, I would straightaway say a big NO.

Next day, the morning happened with the coherence between my phone alarm & chirping of birds. Lying on my bed, I saw the morning through my window and felt like talking to those birds, thanking this entire realm and giving a big hug to my very own self for I was the proudest in the day. From brushing to bathing, everything felt so good that day.

For the last time, I slipped in my office uniform which carried me through everything with sheer loyalty and solely remained my badge of honour to this day. I slipped in my shoes, opened my drawer to collect my watch, ID card and handkerchief. Every little thing mattered as they too had their lasts. Once I got ready, I gave one final look to my entire room for it won't be looked at again with these office-going eyes ever again. I smiled, switched off the lights and locked the door to have one last marathon of catching my bus.

As I made my way towards the bus stop, I saw thousands of my shadows going through this road simultaneously. The one from the early days of 2021 who didn't know where his career was headed, the energetic and enthusiastic one who just got promoted to Deputy manager, the sad and gloomy one who wanted to resign and finally the bravest one who nailed it while finishing the crossing line. When I saw my different personalities simultaneously, I couldn't react but felt a tear in my eye.

The dawn has been taken over by the early morning sun and there couldn't be a better way to describe the stage of my life at the moment. First time in my life, I reached the stop even before the bus' arrival. The bus came in and I got in to have the final journey to my office. Everything had changed that day. The bus, which was usually packed with crowds, was vacant enough to allow me to enjoy the window side alone. I comforted myself and pondered on everything I should have.

By 8 in the morning, I reached the office. I saw no difference in the day except the wicked smile on my close friend's face. He knew how relieved I might be and how I had freed myself from the toxic workplace. Aman sir too was constantly pulling my leg that how lucky I was to get off from this place. For the first hour, it went around in the same fashion but then everyone continued with their work. It's the harsh reality of work life. No one cares to bother, neither about your arrival nor about your departure. It's just your special day. For others, life still sucks.

By the time I finished my lunch, I was done with formalities like returning my laptop, my id's, etc. I was literally roaming empty-handed in the premises of the plant. Every place had a strong memory associated with it.

Some places would make me so emotional that I would almost utter a cry while few would remind me the reason I was leaving this place. Slowly and steadily, I kept on roaming around and meeting people. That day, every person I met would have a big smile on his or her face when I would communicate with them about my departure. It was exactly in the similar fashion as if we all were prisoners and today was my redemption day. They all greeted me with the same vibes "How lucky".

It was already past 2 in the noon and as I anticipated, I was not getting any farewell. My Head hated me and everyone was supposed to listen to him. To be honest, it feels the worst when you don't get a farewell. Although, I saw this coming but my heart had a little hope. I even had a speech prepared and even the list of people I would be grateful to, in my mind. But there was a very little hope.

By the time I was done with all the formalities, I called Mahendra, the guy who supported our department as data entry man, to help me transit back to the warehouse. I was in the plant to greet a few old friends and return my belongings and it was time (3 PM) to return. Mahendra came with his bike and started telling his stories, as he always used to, on the way. "Sir, I really enjoyed working with you. You deserved a farewell!" "No one would give me one, Mahendra ji. Neither I served here for years nor people liked me. And thank you for the appreciation, I too enjoyed working with you."

Close to 3.30 it was and the scorching heat of sun was none less than a hot bath. All drenched in sweat, we reached the warehouse. He went to park his bike while I headed inside my office.

"*Aree akshay sir!!*" Mahendra shouted. With helmet dangling on his one hand, he was swiftly walking towards me to stop. He asked me to come along with him and I followed. He ushered me to an IT maintenance room which was a 10 by 10 small room, mainly equipped with heavy machines and wires. There I could see our IT guy and friends of Mahendra, who all worked in my department as a data support guy.

They wanted to give me a small farewell. Unfortunately they were not white collar workers here but this gesture of them literally gave me a lesson that day. I was almost in tears but somehow controlled. "*Sir, wo log bhale hi aapko farewell na de, ye humari taraf se chota sa gesture*". I can see snacks, cold drinks with a few marigold flower garlands. They wanted to felicitate me in their own style and I couldn't be thankful for them enough. Next, they called Aman sir, who secretly sneaked in the IT room with apologetic eyes (he couldn't give me a farewell). And then started the cutest felicitation ceremony.

Next, I was surrounded by them in photogenic poses with my chest almost covered by garlands. Post the photograph sessions, we had cold drinks and snacks with loads of conversation. They gave me a diary and pen. I seriously didn't know how they got to know that I was fond of writing and journaling. It was a very sweet gesture. After the smallest farewell ceremony, we went back to our tables.

This was going to be my last walk towards my desk. I looked around the entire warehouse, the barrened terrace, the helpless workers, the forklifts, the machinery, the unsettled food mess, the painful eyes yet smiling faces, everything. I wanted to bow down once. Not because it was my first job or because I learnt a lot here but this place transformed me into a MAN. The 22 year old boy who first entered this place was no more than a newbie. There were a lot of takeaways and I couldn't be more proud of it.

The last legendary walk from the warehouse to my desk took me almost an eternity to reach my workstead. I entered my office for the one last time, from the back gate.

As I entered , I saw the chaos of people still fighting over spare parts. Amidst the chaos, I saw the shadow of a 22 year old myself entering the office from the first gate. Anxious but curious, he's looking here and there and probably thinking about his upcoming life in this warehouse. I am almost telepathing him from the other end, assuring him that everything's going to be well. He looks back, gives a smile and vanishes. The reality hits back.

It's more than 4 in the noon and we are close to 5.30. I can feel the sound every time the clock is ticking a second.

I am observing and feeling every bit of my surroundings. My old diaries, the sticky notes, water bottle, coffee cups, desk, bottle, bag. It's time to wrap everything. I am writing an emotional note now. For the one last time, an email to my office colleagues,

"There is no such thing as bad weather. Only different types of good weather. I am accepting both the sides as good weather.

Team VECV, by 1731Hrs today, consider me as your ex-colleague. Please accept a thank you note to each and every one of you for being an integral part of my journey."

And sent.

5.15 the clock struck and everyone started to wrap. People are excited to head back home while I am headed to put a full stop to my first job. Forgetting the pain of not being at the receiving end of a decent farewell, I started greeting everyone for the one last time. With a jolly face, everyone is greeting me back and wishing me fortune for my upcoming life. For the one last time, my colleague Sarthak is taking a selfie with me in the premises of the warehouse. I don't know how to react in the selfie photographs but I am somehow managing to give a smile.

And for the one final time, I am headed back to board the company's bus. Aman Verma and his colleague Naresh, who is also in a similar position, are discussing something about me on the bus. I am getting the gist of their planning a farewell for me. "Akshay, don't go to silicon city today. Come to Vijaynagar with Sarthak. Time to celebrate!" Aman sir urged me to come.

Vijayanagar was the posh area in the city unlike the Silicon city where I lived due to its close proximity to my place.

Having evening plans with Aman & Naresh, I headed to Vijay Nagar along with Sarthak and Vishwas. To be honest, it was a very tough ride for me. I never wanted to leave this organisation in such a fashion. No matter how toxic this job was, it was always special being the first of my career. My career started here where I saw umpteen ups & downs followed by some very good memories with my friends and my flatmates. Everything was happening in such a quick manner that it was becoming very tough for me to both observe and absorb every single detail of that day. I was looking outside the window and seeing a play of memories of the days I spent there. I would see tears, I would see happy faces. It was a mixed emotion.

The entire ride, I kept on blabbering to Sarthak about how I was feeling. He was patiently listening to everything and trying to cheer up how I have got myself out of this situation and would soon be landing in a very good job. My whole life is going to take a turn and that I should be happy and proud of today. Within some 40 minutes, we reached Sarthak's stop i.e. Vijay Nagar. The bus usually stopped at D-Mart there.

As soon as we boarded off the bus, three of us walked around the streets, entered Dmart to buy some stuff and do our regular shenanigans. We encountered that credit card sales guy, whom I was ghosting for many days. He was very adamant today to convince me to buy his card but my emotions were so high that I wasn't in a situation to play around him. I casually told him that it's my last day in Indore. To which, he innocently replied, "This credit card works everywhere, bhaiya." There was a silence for a moment followed by a series of laughter. My mood was finally refreshed and I was laughing openly like a kid now.

The evening dusked beautifully that night. Both the seniors, Aman & Naresh were about to reach anytime. Sarthak and Vishwas were getting ready for the big party while I didn't even change my plant uniform. Obviously I could have borrowed Sarthak's clothes for he was of the same physique as I was but I chose to remain in my blue uniform that night. The uniform stayed to remain loyal to me for some 600 days, why can't I carry it for another night?

It was some 8 in the night when both Aman & Naresh, came in an SUV to pick three of us. The first thing they noticed was I was still in my uniform. Aman sir never leaves the chance to pull my leg. He teased Sarthak, *"Aree, akshay ko ache kapde toh pehna dete?"*. Sarthak threw back some low key banter too.

We continued such banter while in the car and finally reached the top of the cafe. I was the only one dressed in blue uniform while the other four in the group were so handsomely dressed. One might think how awkward and under confident I would be feeling dressed like that at an expensive cafe. To be honest, I wasn't. I was super happy and super proud of myself. One could easily sense the serenity in my eyes and calmness in my gait. I was feeling as if some 100 kgs was taken off my head and I was ready to fly.

We ordered Indian cuisine. It was the first time we five, even after holding a good bond, were sitting together outside the office. I can finally feel the farewell vibes now. With seniors like Aman and Naresh and colleagues like Vishwas and Sarthak, I felt blessed to have them on my farewell. We talked about past events, mocked our bosses, laughed remembering some funny events and continued this for another hour. After getting done with food, all the 5 men took photographs with me being the centre of attraction. Through my photographs, anyone can sense my happiness. I was happy after a very long time. Perhaps, I was proud of my journey.

The night finally came to an end. Aman sir dropped us at the same place where he picked us from. They both didn't bid a bye seated from the car. Aman sir shared his blessings and congratulated me for my journey, *"Bahut maza aaya aapke saath kaam karke!"* while Naresh sir in his own style greeted me, "It was a pleasure working with you Akshay. God bless you!".

With that, not just the evening but my entire journey of my first job came to an end. We reached Sarthak's flat and retired ourselves in the room.

Life was gonna change for both of them too. Vishwas was going to fill in my shoes and Sarthak had to continue his job without his colleague now. They both were very tired and soon went to sleep.

I stood alone in the balcony for some time and gradually slept in the balcony itself with my uniform on.